YOUR KNOWLEDGE H

Do Hai Dang Le

Effectiveness and limitations of IT-based business simulation games

GRIN Verlag

Bibliografische Information der Deutschen Nationalbibliothek:

Die Deutsche Bibliothek verzeichnet diese Publikation in der Deutschen National-
bibliografie; detaillierte bibliografische Daten sind im Internet über http://dnb.d-
nb.de/ abrufbar.

Imprint:

Copyright © 2012 GRIN Verlag GmbH
Druck und Bindung: Books on Demand GmbH, Norderstedt Germany
ISBN: 978-3-656-54330-5

This book at GRIN:

http://www.grin.com/en/e-book/264695/effectiveness-and-limitations-of-it-based-
business-simulation-games

GEORG-AUGUST-UNIVERSITÄT GÖTTINGEN

CHAIR OF APPLICATION SYSTEMS AND E-BUSINESS

SEMINAR ON BUSINESS INFORMATICS, INFORMATICS

AND BUSINESS ECONOMICS

Summer semester 2012

Effectiveness and limitations of IT-based business simulation games

Do Hai Dang Le

Business informatics

7th Semester

Table of contents

List of abbreviations

CBT   computer-based training

E-Learning   electronic learning

IT   information technology

1   Introduction

"You need a game to get the horse to water, but if you keep up an excitement of play, the horse may not drink anything".

- Dr. Sivasailam "Thiagi" Thiagarajan -

Simulation gaming has a long history, which can be traced back to ancient China about 5000 years ago (cf. Faria et al. 2009, p. 465). In modern days, as a relatively new instructional method, it has received much attention from researchers and practitioners. However, as the attention grows, the debate on its effectiveness also becomes louder. Although the aforecited words of Thiagi, an internationally recognized expert in learning games for personal and company, does reveal the most crucial promise and limitation of simulation game, it is only one part of the debate.

By thoroughly reviewing current literatures, this paper will try to address the current dissention on the effectiveness of simulation games and provide a clearer and completer explanation to Thiagi's assertion. However, because this paper is produced within the seminar on business informatics, informatics and business economics, the focus of this paper will be set slightly on one form of simulation game: IT-based business simulation game.

The paper contains four sections. The first part will provide background information to help understanding the focus of this paper by explaining firstly what simulation games are and how they are used in business education and training, as well as how they are supported by IT technologies. Moreover, the process of simulation gaming will also mentioned. In the second part, several the classification of learning outcomes will be introduced to provide additional information and set a framework for the later assessment of the instructional method. The third and the fourth part are the main sections of the paper. In these parts, correspondingly, arguments on the effectiveness and limitations of IT-based business simulation game will be mentioned, along with theoretical and empirical supports.

2   What are IT-based business simulation games?

Because "business simulation game" belongs to a wider, more general concept of simulation gaming, the first part of this section is dedicated to defining simulation game by explaining how it is related to the two more familiar terms "simulation" and "game" and how it inherits the characteristics of these two concepts. The second part will focus on the use of simulation games in business education and training. The process of deploying business simulation games in learning context will be shortly mentioned in the third part. And the fourth section will explain how modern business simulation games are supported by IT technologies.

2.1   Simulation game

In spite of simulation game's long history, among the literatures about simulation and gaming up till now, there is an abundance of works to define and identify the characteristics of simulation games (cf. Garris et al. 2002, p. 442). And many of the existing literatures emphasizes that it is necessary to understand two terms "simulation" and "game" before defining simulation game.

The definition of simulation should begin with its foundation, the model. A model is "a representation of the reality it is constructed to depict" (Feinstein et al. 2002, p. 734). Thus a computer simulation can be defined as an attempt to replicate the characteristics of a system through the use of mathematics or simple object representations (cf. Feinstein et al. 2002, p. 737). Curth (1989, p. 28) mentioned three types of simulation:

- Person-person simulation involves interactions between one or more people. Hand-scored simulation games which will be mentioned later in section 2.4 belong to this type of simulation.
- Person-machine simulation involves interactions between people and computer programs. In this process, user gives inputs and the computer uses these inputs to calculate results and returns feedbacks, which requires user's responses in form of new inputs. Modern computer-based simulation games are examples of this form.
- Machine simulation is similar to person-machine simulation but does not require user's input during the simulation process. Examples of this type

include, among others, simulations of scientific processes such as physical or chemical reactions.

Game consists of "interactions among groups of players (decision makers) placed in a prescribed setting and constrained by a set of rules and procedures" (Hsu 1989, p. 409). Gaming may "involve competition, cooperation, conflict or even collusion" (Hsu 1989, p. 409). Garris et al. (2002, p. 447 ff.) characterized six following features of game:

- Fantasy: games involve imaginary contexts and every action taken place in a game is contained in the virtual world of that game and has no impact on the real world.

- Rules and goals: in spite of being apart from the real world, games also have rules, which govern the gameplay and shape the goal structure of the game.

- Sensory stimuli: since games reflect virtual systems apart from the real world, they enable the experience of unfamiliar sensations or perceptions.

- Challenge: although the goals of a game have to be specific, yet it should not be so easy to achieve. It is the possibility of reaching the goals that decides the degree of challenge of the game.

- Mystery: mystery is created by the discrepancy and inconsistency in information and the complexity, the novelty and the surprise of the game. An adequate degree of mystery of a game arouses the curiosity in the individuals and encourages the desire to obtain more knowledge.

- Control: in instructional contexts, learning contents can be fully controlled by a program or can be partially controlled by learner, which gives learners a degree in which they can control what and how they learn.

By citing Crookall/Saunders (1989, p. 12) and Crookall et al. (1987, p. 151 ff.), Garris et al. (2002, p. 443) suggested that the most important distinction between simulations and games is that simulation tends to represent a real-world system to some extends and game does not. However, the two concepts "simulation" and "game" are not clearly differentiated (cf. Sitzmann 2011, p. 492). Instead, there is a continuous spectrum, with "simulation" on one end and "game" on the other end (cf. Read/Kleiner 1996, p. 27). For that reason, the term "simulation game" may be used best to describe the hybrid instructional tools that stand in the middle of the simulation-game spectrum and inherit the aspects of both simulation and game (cf. Sitzmann 2011, p. 492). In general, a simulation game can be defined as an interactive instructional tool that involves the representation of a real-world system and can contain game characteristics.

2.2 Application fields of simulation game

Historically, simulation games have been used in "specific scientific disciplines (engineering, bio-sciences) and for high-risk occupational training (military, aviation, medicine)" (Jackson 2004, p. 22). In modern days, the use of simulation games has extended far beyond these traditional fields. Randel et al. (1993, p. 264 ff.) conducted a research on the applications of simulation games in many subjects of public education, ranging from social sciences to natural sciences and arts. Furthermore, Jackson (2004, p. 24) also mentioned the deployment of such games for political and religious purposes.

This paper, however, focuses more on business simulation game, or in short, business simulation, which is a subset of simulation game. Fripp (1997, p. 138) discussed business simulation games and stated that most of them have the same structure, which, like other types of simulation, involves the representation of a real or hypothetical business environment where players can compete. Moreover, these games usually require players to develop products or services and make various comprehensive decisions and actions. The statement given by Fripp is used in this paper as a definition for business simulation game.

2.3 The business simulation gaming process

The process of deploying business simulation games consists of 3 phases: the briefing phase, the playing phase and the debriefing phase, which can be summarized as follows (cf. Orth 1997, p. 30 ff.).

In the *briefing phase*, learners should familiarize themselves with the modeled world in the game, including its rules and goals, as well as some general information such as the purpose and structure of the course.

The *playing phase* is the main part of the game and is divided into several rounds; each represents a modeled period of time in the game world. If it is the first period, learners have to analyze the starting situation and, by reference to the game goals, construct a game strategy, which set the guidelines for later decisions. After decisions are made at the end of each round, they will be evaluated and their effects will be presented. Then learners will have to analyze the effects of their last decisions as well as the actualized situation to adjust their strategies and make new decisions. In general, by adjusting their decisions in each round of the game and observing the consequent results, participants have the ability to experiment with and explore the simulated system.

During the *debriefing phase*, learners emerge from the game world and discuss with each other to review their experiences and impressions. Then they begin examining the simulation model which they just played to identify the equivalence between the modeled and the real world. In the last step of the debriefing phase, learners only focus on the equivalences they already identified and consider which experiences to be relevant to them and will be kept and applied after the course (cf. Steinwachs 1992, p. 187).

2.4 The influence of IT on business simulation game

Early business games were hand-scored by instructors. This imposed limitations on the complexity of the model and also on the number of variables included, the number of participants and the number of products and markets in the game world (cf. Fritzsche/Burns 2001, p. 86). Moreover, the workloads of participants and instructors while playing hand-scored games were high which resulted in various kinds of errors (cf. Faria et al. 2009, p. 469).

As business school started to adopt mainframe computers and along with the introduction and the pervasion of microcomputers, the mentioned limitations were removed. Many business games were migrated to these platforms and even more have been newly developed exclusively for microcomputers (cf. Fritzsche/Burns 2001, p. 90). There are general and particular features that the microcomputer contributes to simulation game. The general features include, among others, lower cost, better accessibility, better user-friendliness and easier software installation and administration (cf. Fritzsche/Burns 2001, p. 90). Particularly for simulation games, microcomputers with their increasing computation capability allow the construction of more complex models, which consequently increases the number of participants, and the level of detail of the games (cf. Faria et al. 2009, p. 469). Furthermore, the enhanced graphical user interface in microcomputers enables audio-visual contents to be embedded in programs and support all phases of the business gaming process by, for instance, giving graphical instructions or providing more detailed feedbacks (cf. Faria et al. 2009, p. 469). This generation of business simulation game can be regarded as computer-based business simulation game and is related to computer-based training.

More recently, the growing Internet medium has given even more impetus to business games and thus, many games have been made to exploit the advantages of the Internet. In general, the Internet medium provides communication and interaction across time and distance, as well as access to online resources and most important of all, both two features are available together and economically (cf. Martin 2004, p. 27). Particularly for simulation games, first, the Internet allows new distribution methods of business simulation games such as client-server model using fat clients or web-based clients. The Internet also enables new communication channels which remove spatial and temporal limitations between learners and instructors, such as instant messaging services or conference calling services (cf. Rainey/Lawlor-Wright 2011, p. 3 ff.). All of the features provided above enable the international distribution and participation in business simulationg games. This generation of business simulation games can be called internet-based or web-based business simulation games. Moreover, as internet-based simulation game is an instructional tool aided by the Internet, it is reasonable to suggest that it is one of many E-Learning methods.

To summarize this section, a conclusion can be drawn that business simulation game is one among many application fields of a wider concept of simulation gaming, which inherits characteristics of both simulation and game. Throughout its development, under the influence of IT, business simulation game has evolved from old hand-scored games through mainframe-based and computer-based games into modern internet-based business simulation games.

In this paper, the term "IT-based business simulation game" refers to both computer-based and internet-based business simulation games. Since hand-scored games are not the focus of this paper, it is a redundancy to repeatedly use the term "IT-based business simulation games", instead, the shorter terms "business simulation games" or "business simulations" will be used in several places. Moreover, in later parts of this paper, when the term "simulation game" is used, it means the mentioned points are valid to simulation games in general and thus they should also be valid to business simulation games in particular. Beside general issues of simulation games, particular issues of IT-based business simulation games will also be mentioned.

3 What can be affected by IT-based business simulation games?

Since the main purpose of this paper is to identify the effectiveness and limitations of IT-based business simulation games on learners and since IT-based simulation game is an instructional method, the effectiveness as well as limitations mentioned in this paper should focus mostly on learning outcomes. Thus, in this section, a classification of learning outcomes will be introduced to set a framework for the next section.

In 1993, Kraiger et al. proposed a conceptual classficication, in which learning outcomes are divided into three categories: cognitive, skill-based and affective outcomes (cf. Kraiger et al. 1993, p. 312 ff.).

Cognitive outcomes consist of three levels: verbal knowledge, knowledge organization and cognitive strategies.

- *Verbal knowledge* is categorized into three stages. Declarative knowledge refers to facts and data required to complete a task (the "what"). Procedural knowledge refers to knowledge about how to perform a task (the "how"). Strategic knowledge is the application of learned knowledge in different contexts and situations and the derivation of more knowledge for general situation (the "which, when, why") (cf. Garris et al. 2002, p.456). It should be noticed that these knowledge stages have to be obtained successively, which means declarative knowledge has to precede the other two stages.
- *Knowledge organization* involves grouping pieces of knowledge into a mental model to be stored in long-term memory. As learners begin to expertize the task, their memory starts being organized by forming interrelationships between components of the model. This process takes place when learners start to gain procedural knowledge.

- Finally, as knowledge has been gained and organized, *cognitive strategies* are developed and are ready to be applied in different situations. The result of this process is strategic knowledge.

Skill-based outcomes include the development of technical and motor stages and are, like cognitive outcomes, divided into three successive stages, which can be achieved only by continuous training (cf. Garris et al. 2002, p. 455; cf. Kraiger et al. 1993, p. 317):

- *Initial skill acquisition* begins with the process of transforming declarative knowledge to procedural knowledge, in which learners learn how to perform a task.
- *Skill compilation* involves practicing trained behaviors and allows faster performance with less error.
- *Skill automaticity* enables not only a quick but also personalized performance of the tasks. After reaching automaticity stage, learners can not only perform the task fluidly, but also perform it parallel and in combination with other tasks.

Affective outcomes are also categorized into two subsets: attitudinal and motivational outcomes.

- Attitude is defined as how a person evaluates something and serves as a predisposition that can affect that person's performance (cf. Arias-Aranda/Bustinza-Sánchez 2009, p. 1106). *Attitude outcomes* refer to changes in learners's attitudes on various objects and topics.
- *Motivational outcomes* include motivational disposition, self-efficacy and goal setting. Motivational disposition may encourage learners to increase their own knowledge in a specific field to perform the task better. Self-efficacy is one's personal perception of his own ability and capability to perform a specific task and can influence his choice of task, his persistence and amount of effort given and his performance. Goal setting, like self-efficacy, also influence the persistence of effort and the extent to which knowledge and skills learned in the course will be applied to real life.

4 Why are IT-based business simulation games good?

Throughout its development, a lot of researches regarding the effectiveness of IT-based business simulation game have been conducted, both theoretically and empirically. As IT-based business simulation game is an instructional method, it is necessary to mention firstly its effects on learners' learning outcomes, then on other aspects.

4.1 Effectiveness on learning outcomes of participants

As already described in section 3, learning outcomes are categorized into cognitive outcomes, skill-based outcomes and affective outcomes. For that reason, this section will also be divided into three corresponding parts.

4.1.1 Affective outcomes

The first to be attended are affective outcomes which include changes in learners' attitudes and motivation (cf. Kraiger et al. 1993, p. 318 ff.).

Attitude is the internal state that influences the performance and behaviors of individuals (cf. Gagné 1984, p. 383). Recent literature tends to concentrate on changes in learners' attitude toward the simulation game and toward their perceived learning. Wolfe (1985, p. 279) stated: "games appear to change attitudes about the games themselves and what the participants think about their experiences". Researches of Remus/Jenner (1979, p. 83) and Anderson/Lawton (2009, p. 196) also reported that learners showed a generally positive attitude toward the simulation games over other instructional methods such as lectures or case discussions.

Nevertheless, there are concerns about the validity of researches on the attitudinal outcomes. Anderson/Lawton (2009, p. 196), while confirmed the positive change in attitude of learners toward simulation games, argued that previous researches which attempted to measure learners' attitudinal changes toward their learning relied only on self-reports from participants and are therefore not objective enough. Wolfe (1985, p. 279) expressed another concern that some measured attitudinal changes correlate to learners' end-game ranking and are very questionable. This concern is reasonable, because when learners achieve a high performance in courses with simulation games, which is expressed subjectively by a high note or a high rank at the end of the game, they tend to show positive attitude toward simulation games and regard them as an effective instructional method.

As for motivation, many theories support the claims of the motivational effectiveness of business simulations. First, the theory of Malone (1981, p. 335 ff.) assumes that business simulation game is itself "intrinsically motivating" because it possesses all the required characteristics: challenge, fantasy and curiosity. Garris et al.'s (2002, p. 445 ff.) input-process-outcome theory also suggested that a right mix between instructional contents and game characteristics of simulation games may keep learners involving in the gaming process till the end of the game. Tennyson/Jorczak (2008, p. 7) also remarked that simulations games are excel at engaging both affective and cognitve system of participants and thus, according to their Interactive Cognitive Complexity theory, will increase their motivation and learning. Besides, their theory also suggested the importance of sensory information in the learning process, which can be stimulated by IT-based simulation games by utilizing audial and visual features of computer technologies as mentioned in the "sensory stimuli" characteristic of games.

Empirical evidence founded in several studies also give credence to the theories. Venkatesh/Speier (2000, p. 995 ff.) studied the effectiveness of game-based training on business teleworkers and concluded that those who have undergone such training achieve a higher level of motivation than others. Surveys taken by Waggener (1979, p. 115) and Wawer et al. (2010, p. 67) also reported a significant motivational advantage of business simulation games with correspondingly 82% and 96% surveyed students favoring this method. Researches were also taken to measure the effects of audio-visual features of computer simulation games on learners' motivation and showed specifically that when both visual and verbal feedbacks are given in the game, learners are less frustrated and more interested in the game (Rieber et al. 2004, p. 317 ff.).

Beside motivational disposition, changes in learner's self-efficacy had also been observed in a number of studies which were summarized by Sitzmann (2011, p. 495 f.). Accordingly, since simulation games use models to imitate real-world systems, participants have the chance to enhance their experience in work-related tasks. This creates the feeling that they will be able to perform the tasks well in real situations. Moreover, simulation games provide trainees with a virtual environment to apply and evaluate their knowledge base and skills. As a result, they tend to achieve a high level of self-efficacy because they already have their knowledge and skill proven in the games. Last but not least, the high interactivity of business simulation games as well as the ability to make decisions make learners feel empowered and consequently increase their self-efficacy. Sitzmann's (2011, p. 520) meta-analysis also provided empirical data that those who learned through simulation games achieve 20% higher self-efficacy than those who used traditional training methods.

4.1.2 Skill-based outcomes

Generally, simulation games allow the repetitive practice of performing any task which is a prerequisite to skill improvement as mentioned in section 3. Thus, it can be assumed that simulation gaming increases learners' skills because when learners are motivated and keep practicing repetitively, the process of skill compilation and then skill automaticity will take place and thus, learners will perform that task more fluidly and correctly.

Positive effects of simulation games on the improvement of learners' technical skills have been reported in several researches on simulations (cf. Wilson et al. 2009, p. 253 f.). In addition, effects on specific job skills such as personnel administration, hiring, motivating, leading or research and data analysis were also reported to be positive (cf. Faria 2001, p. 103). Beside technical skills (or "hard" skills), a number of managerial skills (or "soft" skills) can also be improved by using simulation games. A survey taken by Teach/Govahi (1988, p. 70) on business managers who had attended simulation game courses while students concluded that business simulation games are regarded to be the most effective way to teach several managerial skills such as objective measuring, problem solving and forecasting. In addition, there are also claimes of positive effects on skills such as leadership, decision-making, systematic thinking, conflict management, communication and team work (cf. Greenblat 1973, p. 67; cf. Whitton/Hynes 2006; cf. Faria 2001, p. 103; cf. Arias-Aranda/Bustinza-Sánchez 2009, p. 1106).

4.1.3 Cognitive outcomes

Since business simulation game is an instructional method, improving participants' knowledge base should be its main purpose. The Interactive Cognitive Complexity theory of Tennyson/Jorczak (2008, p. 7) suggests that simulation games should produce better cognitive outcomes, because they allow the interaction between learners' affects and knowledge base. Empirical analyses also agree with this assumption.

Randel et al. (1993, p. 263 ff.) analysed a number of studies from 1963 to 1984 on the effectiveness on cognitive gain and knowledge retention of simulations and games and noted that although there is a difference between various subjects, in social sciences which include business education there is an advantage of simulation games over traditional methods. Although the actuality of this meta-analysis can be doubted, it covered such a wide range of studies that its results are still be cited today. Similar results favoring simulation games were also founded in other meta-analyses (cf. Vogel et al. 2006, p. 235; cf. Sitzmann 2011, p. 508). Particularly Sitzmann (2011, p. 508) reported specifically that learners using simulation games obtain a higher level of declarative knowledge (11%), procedural knowledge (14%) as well as retention (9%) than those using traditional teaching methods. In term of business education and training, Blunt also reviewed three studies on the use of three simulation games on business, economics and managements in an US university and also found the advantages in learning achievements of all three games (cf, Blunt 2007, p. 949 ff.).

However, while many studies pointed out the advantages of using simulation games regarding cognitive outcomes, there are also objections. Anderson/Lawton reviewed a number of studies up to 2007 and identified two reasons (2009, p. 200 ff.). The first reason is that what has been measured so far is only knowledge at the lowest stage, which is declarative and procedural knowledge. This argument is also supported by Wilson et al. by stating that "within the cognitive arena, there was one area that dominated much of the research examining game attributes and outcomes: declarative knowledge" (Wilson et al. 2009, p. 235). The second reason is that the analysis methods used so far are limited to self-reports of participants, which can only measure what participants think they have learned, not what they have really learned.

As a conclusion for this section, it can be concluded that although there are theoretical and empirical credence to the positive effectiveness of simulation games on learners's cognitive outcomes, the results are still controversial. For that reason, an argument of Anderson/Lawton (2009, p. 200) can be used: "We have a long way to go to provide objective evidence of the learning efficacy of business simulation exercises".

4.2 Effectiveness on other aspects of education and training

In addition to the learning outcomes of participants described above which are derived from the nature of simulation game, there are several other advantages of IT-based simulation games which have also been observed. These advantages are either derived from the nature of simulation game or from the support of IT.

First, the application of IT to this instructional method enables flexible training, with saves students a lot of time and effort. With the old hand-scored or mainframe-based simulation games, students had to be present at campus to submit their decisions in written form and to receive feedback from instructors. Even at the beginning of the computer era, without the Internet, student still had to personally submit their decision in diskettes. The Internet relieves them from this time-consuming process by enable the submission of game decisions via electronic mail or by using File Transfer Protocol and most recently via direct communication between game client and server (cf. Peach/Platt 1998, p. 46 ff.; cf. Thavikulwat/Chang 2007, p. 114 f.). Another aspect of flexible training is that participants and instructors do not have to be present at the class or meet each other face-to-face. They can instead use Internet communication tools such as electronic mail, social network pages, instant messaging services or conference calling services for the purpose (cf. Rainey/Lawlor-Wright 2011, p. 3 ff.). Moreover, like other CBT and E-Learning methods, flexible learning also results in the ability of trainees to decide the place, the time and the pace of their learning, which may increase the mobility of learning and positively affect the learning outcomes. Modern web-based simulation games which do not require any installation also add to this advantage. An example is an employee who travels to a real-world negotiation session can practice negotiating using a simulation game installed in his computer (cf. Summers 2004, p. 227).

Second, the use of computer as a scoring platform and the internet as a submission method effectively reduces the workloads of game instructors and the risk of media disruption during the gaming process. In the early years of simulation game, as learners' decision had to be submitted in written form and hand-scored by instructors, various kinds of errors might occur. For example, students might mistakenly write down false numbers or instructors might read or score the results wrongly or input wrong numbers to the scoring computer (cf. Faria et al. 2009, p. 469). Newer simulation games which ran on computers allowed participants to submit their decisions in diskettes, which diminished the risk of error and relieved instructors from manually entering inputs for game program (cf. Faria et al. 2009, p. 469). Modern IT-based simulation games allow a direct transfer of users' inputs and system feedbacks between clients and servers which effectively eliminates some sources of errors. Moreover, modern games are scored exclusively by the computer and thus, they relieve instructors of the burden of scoring the game.

Last but not least, specifically for business administrators who wish to use simulation games to train their employees and also for individual simulation game users, computer-bases business simulation is a cost-effective training method. Standard simulations nowadays are developed so that they can be tailored to meet specific customers' needs meanwhile maintaining lower price (cf. Summers 2004, p. 217). Moreover, using business simulation games as a training method reduces or eliminates costs associated with training delivery such as participants' traveling and accommodation costs, and the compensation for their lost productivity during their absence. It was estimated that such indirect costs can amount to 80% of the total training cost (cf. Kozlowski et al. 2001, p. 60). Thus using IT-based simulation games helps companies managing their training budget more effectively (cf. Sitzmann, 2011, p. 514).

This section has provided some evidence on the effectiveness of IT-based business simulation games on multiple aspects, although in some cases the effects are still controversial. However, just as other instructional methods, IT-based business simulation game is not flawless. It still has some issues and limitations which will be mentioned in the following section.

5.   How can IT-based business simulation games fail?

Contrary to the vast number of studies on the effectiveness of simulation games, there are few focusing on their limitations. However, since there is a relation between IT-based simulation game, CBT and E-Learning as already mentioned in section 2.4, a derivation from the issues of CBT and E-Learning seems to be possible. Thus in this sectioned, several issues which might be also valid to IT-based simulation games will be selectively mentioned. In general, the issues concerning the use of IT-based business simulation games stem from the nature of simulation game, from the gaming process, from the limitations regarding technologies and from the learners themselves (cf. Wong 2007, p. 55 ff.; cf. Hofstede et al. 2010, p. 839 f.). Thus, this section will be conrespondingly divided into four parts. Moreover, it can be recognized that while the first two issues relate to general simulation games, the second two only appear along with the application of IT technologies in simulation games.

5.1   Issues from the nature of simulation game

Since the model and the game characteristic are the major components of any simulation game, Hofstede et al. (2010, p. 834 f.) mentioned three possibile threats concerning the choice of a suitable model and the implementation of game features in the simulation games. First, if the designer uses a right model, but failed to make it enjoyable due to lack of motivating features, the game will fail to motivate learners and thus, learners will not actively take part in the game or stay with the game till the end. Second, if the designer chooses a wrong model, but the game is still enjoyable, learners will still enjoy the game, but they fail to obtain the desired learning outcomes. And finally, if the model is right and the game is enjoyble, game facilitators still have to assure that learners obtain the desired learning outcomes and know how to use them which raises other issues concerning the debriefing phase and the game instructors.

Moreover, as simulation game is a simplified representation of a real-world system, many aspects of the real world are missing. One example is the process of decision enforcement which is lacking in business simulation games, as the games only require learners to make decisions, submit them and response to system feedbacks (cf. Curth 1989, p. 27). Besides, decisions taken in games have no consequence in real life, there is a possible threat that learners may not take their decisions and the results of their decisions seriously and responsibly (cf. Read/Kleiner 1996, p. 27; cf. Wawer et al. 2010, p. 66).

5.2 Issues during the gaming process

During the gaming process, there is a consensus in most literatures on the need for competent game instructors. There are at least three reasons for the argument.

First, during gameplay, socio-emotional problems may happen. In particular, inferior participant might be so frustrated that they may quit the game or superior participants may pursue aggressive tactics to force others to quit. Such problems not only have to be prevented by instructors but should also be used to contribute to the game evaluation later (cf. Hofstede et al. 2010, p. 839 f.).

Second, cross-cultural issues may also occur and interfere with the learning outcomes, especially when either the game designers, the participants or the instructors are from different cultures. One example was an old American board game named "So long sucker" (cf. Hofstede/Murff 2012, p. 43 f.). The game requires players to form diplomatic alliances with each other and eliminate weaker players and would normally take a few minutes. However, when the game was played by Taiwanese students, they took extensive considerations and were reluctant to eliminate each other, which lengthened game duration and resulted in an undesired outcome (cf. Hofstede/Murff 2012, p. 43 f.). In this case, even the experienced instructor, who for the first time experienced this phenomena, doubted the competence of herself (cf. Hofstede et al. 2010, p. 837).

Third, game instructors also have to faciliate the debriefing process which, as already mentioned in section 2.3, helps learners understanding the relationships between the game and real-life world and knowing how to apply what they have learned. This phase is perhaps the most important in the business gaming process, yet it is the most neglected, not only in the literature, but also in practice (cf. Crookall 1992, p. 141). Because of its importance, it can be realized that if it is poorly facilitated by incompetent instructors, learners will not understand which knowledge should be kept after the game and how to apply it, which may lead to the failure of the game (cf. Lederman 1992, p. 145).

All three issues mentioned above call for the presence of competent instructors. Yet instructing a simulation game is not only a qualification but a complicated, multifaceted skill, which is hard to obtain (cf. Hofstede et al. 2010, p. 837).

Furthermore, if the gaming process involves the use of online simulation games and does not require participants and instructors to meet each other, it may cause the lack of face-to-face interaction which would make the training less attractive to participants and can reduce its effectiveness (cf. Welsh et al. 2003, p. 249; cf. Bonk et al. 2004, p. 74). Moreover, without any interaction with other people, participants may also suffer from psychologically isolation during the process which has been suggested to the major reason for a high drop-out rates of distance courses (cf. Croft et al. 2010, p. 33). Although such obstacles can be overcome by using groupware technologies such as instant messaging, audio- and videoconferencing or forums, the technologies are resource intensive and still underutilized by learners (cf. Welsh et al. 2003, p. 249; cf. Proserpio/Gioia 2007, p. 77 f.).

Last but not least, there are also other factors which need to be attended during the gaming process. Sitzmann suggested and analysed some of such so-called "moderators" (cf. Sitzmann 2011, p. 489 ff.). First, learners should have unlimited access to the games and should be allowed to utilize them as long as they desires. To explain it, he referred to Garris et al.'s input-process-outcome model and stated that essential time to play the game is a prerequisite for the game cycle to occur and that any limit imposed on learners should interrupt the cycle (cf. Sitzmann 2011, p. 516). Second, the level of activeness of the course have to be considered. Even though the playing phase of the game is itself active, using passive methods in the connecting briefing and debriefing phases may also dillute the effects of simulation games (cf. Sitzmann 2011, p. 517). The last moderator is how to deploy simulation game properly in learning courses, which should be noticed by simulation games facilitators. Simulation games should not be used as a stand-alone instructional methods, because "people do not naturally learn complex relationships from experience alone" (Sitzmann, 2011, p. 515). For that reason, simulation games should be regarded as a supplement, not a substitution to conventional methods (cf. Feldman 1995, p. 358).

5.3 Issues regarding information technology

While IT technoligies are regarded as enabling factors of modern simulation games as stated in section 2.4, they also cause several potential problems regarding the required IT infrastructure and development cost.

Using computer-based simulation games requires access to computers and the Internet. For that reason, the costs for the procurement, installation and maintanance of the required hardware and the acquisition of an Internet connection have to be taken into account (cf. Welsh et al. 2003, p. 249). Moreover, as already mentioned in section 4.2, one of the advantages of using IT-based simulation games is that learners are able to stay at home or stay mobile interacting with the game server and communicating with each other via the Internet. However, in order to turn such abilities into advantanges, first there has to be Internet access and second the Internet connection has to be fast and stable enough (cf. Wong 2007, p. 56). This issue affects not only companies and educational institutes in developing countries (cf. Wong 2007, p. 56), but may also affect learners in industrial countries who want to utilize the mobility in learning.

As for development cost, since the use of computer allows the construction of ever complexer models, the construction of such models also becomes complexer and and requires more resource. It has been estimated that while other E-Learning methods require 220 hours of development for each hour of instructional content, each hour of content in IT-based simulation games require 750 to 1.500 development hours (cf. Summers 2004, p. 228 f.). Although the issue can be overcome by purchasing customizable standard simulation games as already mentioned in 4.2, development costs still pose a major obstacle to companies or instutitutes who wish to develop their own simulation games.

5.4 Learners' personal issues

Beside the objective threats mentioned above, there are also possible issues that lie in the learners themselves.

First of all, as simulation game and IT-based simulation game are relatively new, the unfamiliarity of learners with these instrucional methods may entail several problems. The first problem is down to the motivational and interactive characteristics of simulation game. Due to such characteristics, participants may treat simulation game as a mean of entertainment, not a mean of education and may reject them as an instructional method. This problem was addressed particularly to adult participants, who may have had more experience with traditional learning methods (cf. Wawer et al. 2010, p. 66). Moreover, IT-based simulation game also requires specific IT skills to operate the game and to utilize other supporting technologies such as communication and data sharing softwares. In fact, the lack of IT skills and the unfamiliarity with IT technologies pose a barrier to the gaming process and can frustrate learners, which consequently hinders the effectiveness of the game (cf. Wong 2007, p. 56). Proserpio/Gioia (2007, p. 78) also added to this point that even if learners are accustomed to modern Internet communication tools, whether they can utilize such tools to support the learning is questionable.

Moreover, a new characteristic of IT-based simulation game in comparison to older types of simulation game or other classroom instructional methods is that it allows participants to regulate the time, the place and the pace of their learning. This characteristic has been regarded as one of its advantages but it may also be a source of problems regarding time management and procastination which can be exacerbated by the absence of face-to-face interaction among participants and instructors (cf. Sherry 1995, p. 352). First, learning at a distance is time-consuming and, adding to that, even the time dedicated to learning may be disrupted by other activities and interests in learners' personal life and work. Second, unmotivated or undisciplined learners may be reluctant to keep an adequate pace of the learning process and may consequently fail to achieve succesful results or even have to drop out of the course (cf. Sherry 1995, p. 352). For that reason, successful learning with IT-based simulation game in particular and other distance learning methods in general requires learners' self-control of their learning process in form of autonomy, time management and internal motivation (cf. Sherry 1995, p. 351; cf. Wong 2007, p. 56 f.). External factors such as well-specified tasks, standing supports and feedbacks from instructors at the beginning and during the game should also help monitoring and motivating learners and thus overcome the problem (cf. Laari-Muinonen/Viskari 2009, p. 4.3).

6. Discussion

Although simulation games, and particularly IT-based business simulation games, have been considered to be a generally effective instructional method, researches only converge on the effectiveness on motivational and skill-based outcomes. Effects on other learning outcomes are sighted, but evidence is still controversial. Beside the effectiveness on learning outcomes, there are other advantages of IT-based simulation games given by modern IT technologies. However, many issues concerning the game, the gaming process, the technologies and the participants also need to be attended to maintain the effectiveness of the instructional method.

Still, more work needs to be conducted to provide firm evidence on the effects of business simulation games on cognitive learning. Besides, as experienced during the work on this paper, there is a lack of researches directly on the limitations of simulation game in general and IT-based business simulation game in particular. Thus, more structured researches on this topic are needed.

The various topics mentioned in this paper may not cover all the possible effectiveness and limitations of using computer-based business simulation games as this instructional method is a relatively new one and is still evolving under the influence of changes in business and technologies. In term of business, changes such as new organizational structures, the expansion of organizational boundaries through extensive customer and supplier relationship management or the growing pressure of sustainable management are calling for a renewal of simulation games (cf. Fripp 1997, p. 139 f). In terms of technologies, for instance, the use of computer-agents and the widespread use of handheld devices such as laptops, smartphones and tablets have laid the foundations for agent-based simulation games and pervasive simulation gaming (cf. Faria et al. 2009, p. 470). Thus, in the future, the effects of modern technologies on IT-based business simulation games should continue to be studied.

Reference

Anderson, P.; Lawton, L.: Business simulations and cognitive learning: developments, desires and future directions. In: Simulation & Gaming 40 (2009) 2, pp. 193-216.

Arias-Aranda, D.; Bustinza-Sánchez, O.: Entrepreneurial attitude and conflict management through business simulations. In: Industrial Management & Data Systems 109 (2009) 8, pp. 1101-1117.

Blunt, R.: Does game-based learning work? Results from three recent studies. In: Interservice/Industry Training, Simulation & Education Conference, 2007-11-26 to 2007-11-29, Orlando, USA 2007.

Bonk, C.; Wisher, R.; Lee, J.: Moderating learner-centered e-Learning: Problems and solutions, benefits and implications. In: Roberts, T. (ed.): Online Collaborative Learning: Theory and Practice, Hershey, USA 2004, pp. 55-84.

Croft, N.; Dalton, A.; Grant, M.: Overcoming isolation in distance learning: Building a learning community through time and space. In: Journal for Education in the Built Environment 5 (2010) 1, pp. 27-64.

Crookall, D.: Editorial: Debriefing. In: Simulation & Gaming 23 (1992) 2, pp. 141-142.

Crookall, D.; Oxford, R.; Saunders, D.: Towards a reconceptualization of simulation: From representation. In: Simulation/Games for Learning 17 (1987), pp. 147-171.

Crookall, D.; Saunders, D.: Towards an integration of communication and simulation. In: Crookall, D.; Saunders, D. (eds.): Communication and simulation: From two fields to one theme, Clevedon, UK 1989, pp. 3-29.

Curth, M.: Planspieltechnik und Computer Based Training zur Schulung von Einkäufern im Handel, Bergisch Gladbach, Germany 1989.

Faria, A. J.: The changing nature of business simulation/ gaming research: A brief history. In: Simulation & Gaming 32 (2001) 1, pp. 97-110.

Faria, A. J.; Hutchinson, D.; Wellington, W. J.: Developments in business gaming: A review of the past 40 years In: Simulation & Gaming 40 (2009) 4, pp. 464-487.

Feinstein, A.; Mann, S.; Corsun, D.: Charting the experiential territory: Clarifying definitions and uses of computer simulation, games, and role play. In: Journal of Management Development 21 (2002) 10, pp. 732-744.

Feldman, H.: Computer-based simulation games: A viable educational technique for entrepreneurship classes? In: Simulation & Gaming 26 (1995) 3, pp. 346-360.

Fripp, J.: A future for business simulations? In: Journal of European Industrial Training 21 (1997) 4, pp. 138-142.

Fritzsche, D.; Burns, A.: The role of ABSEL in the development of marketing simulations in college education. In: Simulation & Gaming 32 (2001) 1, pp. 85-96.

Gagné, R.: Learning outcomes and their effects: Useful categories of human performance. In: American Psychologist 39 (1984) 4, pp. 377-385.

Garris, R.; Ahlers, R.; Driskell, J. E.: Games, motivation, and learning: A research and practice model. In: Simulation & Gaming 33 (2002) 4, pp. 441-467.

Greenblat, C.: Teaching with simulation games: A review of claims and evidence. In: Teaching Sociology 1 (1973) 1, pp. 62-83.

Hofstede, G.; de Caluwé, L.; Peters, V.: Why simulation games work- In search of the active substance: A synthesis. In: Simulation & Gaming 41 (2010) 6, pp. 824-843.

Hofstede, G.; Murff, E.: Repurposing an old game for an international world. In: Simulation & Gaming 43 (2012) 1, pp. 34-50.

Hsu, E.: Role-event gaming simulation in management education: A conceptual framework and review. In: Simulation & Gaming 20 (1989) 4, pp. 409-438.

Jackson, M.: Making visible: Using simulation and game environments across disciplines. In: On the Horizon 12 (2004) 1, pp. 22-25.

Kozlowski, S.W.J.; Toney, R.J.; Mullins, M.E.; Weissbein, D.A.; Brown, K.G.; Bell, B.S.: Developing adaptability: A theory for the design of integrated-embedded training systems. In: Salas, E. (ed.): Advances in human performance and cognitive engineering research, Amsterdam, Netherlands 2001, pp. 59-123.

Kraiger, K.; Ford, J.; Salas, E.: Application of cognitive, skill-based and affective theories of learning outcomes to new methods of training evaluation. In: Journal of Applied Psychology 78 (1993) 2, pp. 311-328.

Laari-Muinonen, L.; Viskari, K.: Experiences in teaching international business with business simulation game. In: Innovative Infotechnologies for Science, Business and Education 1 (2009) 6, pp. 4.1-4.5.

Lederman, L.: Debriefing: Toward a systematic assessment of theory and practice. In: Simulation & Gaming 23 (1992) 2, pp. 145-160.

Lee, J.: Effectiveness of computer-based instructional simulation: A meta-analysis. In: International Journal of Instructional Media 26 (1999) 1, pp. 71-85.

Leutner, D.: Guided discovery learning with computer-based simulation games: effects of adaptive and non-adaptive instructional support. In: Learning and Instruction 3 (1993), pp. 113-132.

Malone, T.: Toward a theory of intrinsically motivating instruction. In: Cognitive Science 4 (1981), pp. 333-369.

Malone, T.; Lepper, M.: Making learning fun: A taxonomy of intrinsic motivations for learning. In: Snow, R.; Farr, M. (eds.): Aptitude, learning, and instruction: Vol. 3. Conative and affective. Hillsdale, USA 1987, pp. 223-253.

Martin, A.: Adding value to simulation/games through Internet mediation: The medium and the message. In: Simulation & Gaming 34 (2004) 1, pp. 23-38.

Miesing, P.; Preble, J.: Group processes and performance in a complex business simulation. In: Small Group Research 16 (1985) 3, pp. 325-328.

Neal, D.: Group competitiveness and cohesion in a business simulation. In: Simulation & Gaming 28 (1997) 4, pp. 460-476.

Orth, C.: Unternehmensplanspiele in der betriebswirtschaftliche Aus- und Weiterbildung, Göttingen, Germany 1997.

Peach, E.; Platt, R.: Total enterprise simulations and the Internet, improving student perceptions and simplifying administrative workloads. In: Developments in Business Simulation and Experiential Learning 25 (1998), pp. 44-50.

Proserpio, L.; Gioia, D.: Teaching the virtual generation. In: Academy of Management Learning & Education 6 (2007) 1, pp. 69-80.

Rainey, M.; Lawlor-Wright, T.: Student perspectives on communication: A case study on different methods of communication used by engineering students. In: European Conference on Civil Engineering Education and Training, 2011-11-24 to 2011-11-26, Patras, Greece 2011.

Randel, J.; Morris, B.; Wetzel, C., Whitehill, D.: The effectiveness of games for educational purposes: a review of recent research. In: Simulation & Gaming 23 (1993) 3, pp. 261-276.

Read, C.; Kleiner, B.: Which training methods are effective? In: Management Development Review 9 (1996) 2, pp. 24-29.

Remus, W.; Jenner, S.: Playing business games: Attitudinal differences between students playing singly and as team. In: Simulation & Gaming 10 (1979) 1, pp. 75-85.

Rieber, L.; Tzeng, S.; Tribble, K.: Discovery learning, representation and explanation within a computer-based simulation: finding the right mix. In: Learning and Instruction 14 (2004), pp. 307-323.

Sherry, L.: Issues in distance learning. In: International Journal of Educational Telecommunications 1 (1995) 4, pp. 337-365.

Sitzmann, T.: A meta-analytic examination of the instructional effectiveness of computer-based simulation games. In: Personnel Psychology 64 (2011), pp. 489-528.

Steinwachs, B.: How to Faciliate a Debriefing. In: Simulation & Gaming 23 (1992) 2, pp. 186-195.

Summers, G.: Today's business simulation industry. In: Simulation & Gaming 35 (2004) 2, pp. 208-241.

Teach, R.; Govahi, G.: The role of experiential learning and simulation in teaching managerial skills. In: Developments in Business Simulation & Experiential Exercises 15 (1988), pp. 65-71.

Tennyson, R.; Jorczak, R.: A conceptual framework for the empirical study of instructional games. In: O'Neil, H.; Perez, R. (eds.): Computer games and team and individual learning, Oxford, UK 2008, pp. 39-54.

Thavikulwat, P.; Chang, J.: Applying .NET remoting to a business simulation. In: Developments in Business Simulation and Experiential Learning 34 (2007), pp. 113-118.

Venkatesh, V.; Speier, C.: Creating an effective training environment for enhancing telework. In: International Journal of Human-Computer Studies 52 (2000), pp. 991-1005.

Vogel, J.J.; Vogel, D.S.; Cannon-Bowers, J.; Bowers, C.A.; Muse, K.; Wright, M.: Computer gaming and interactive simulations for learning: A meta-analysis. In: Journal of Educational Computing Research 3 (2006), pp. 229-243.

Waggener, H.: Simulation vs cases vs text: An analysis of student opinion. In: Journal of Experiential Learning and Simulation 1 (1979), pp. 113-118.

Wawer, M.; Milosz, M.; Muryjas, P.; Rzemieniak, M.: Business simulation games in forming of students' entrepreneurship. In: International Journal of Euro-Mediterranean Studies 3 (2010) 1, pp. 49-71.

Wellington, W.; Faria, A.J.: An examination of the effect of team cohesion, player attitude and performance expectations on simulation performance results. In: Developments In Business Simulation & Experiential Exercises 19 (1992), pp. 184-189.

Welsh, E.; Wanberg, C.; Brown, K.; Simmering, M.: E-learning: emerging uses, empirical results and future directions. In: International Journal of Training and Development 7 (2003) 4, pp. 245-258.

Whitton, N.; Hynes, N.: Evaluating the effectiveness of an online simulation to teach business skills. http://www.ascilite.org.au/ajet/e-jist/docs/vol9_no1/papers/current_practice/whitton_hynes.htm, 2006, accessed on 2012-05-08.

Wilson, K.A.; Bedwell, W.L.; Lazzara, E.H.; Salas, E.; Burke, C.S.; Estock, J.L.; Orvis, K.L.; Conkey, C.: Relationships between game attributes and learning outcomes: Reviews and research proposals. In: Simulation & Gaming 40 (2009) 2, pp. 217-266.

Wolfe, J.: The teaching effectiveness of games in collegiate business courses: A 1973-1983 update. In: Simulation & Gaming 16 (1985) 3, pp. 251-288.

Wolfe, J.: A history of business teaching games in English-speaking and post-socialist countries: The origination and diffusion of a management education and development technology. In: Simulation & Gaming 24 (1993) 4, pp. 446-463.

Wolfe, J.; Crookall, D.: In memoriam. In: Simulation & Gaming 24 (1993) 2, pp. 7-8.

Wong, D.: A critical literature review on E-Learning limitations. In: Journal of the Advancement of Science & Arts 2 (2007), pp. 55-62.